The Oxford Kilburn Youth Trust

Annual Report 2016-17

The OK Club, 45 Denmark Road, London NW6 5BP

www.okclub.org.uk

Registered charity in England and Wales number 1099564

A company limited by guarantee, registered in England & Wales 04323224

Published December 2017

© The Oxford Kilburn Youth Trust

The short version

We've worked with **285** different children and young people and we've seen an increase in attendance of **40%** on the previous year. During the year we ran **639** hours of youth and children's work. And we balanced the books.

Introduction

The OK Club works with young people and their families in Kilburn, North-West London. We work with them to build character and capabilities, as they grow into active and engaged adults. We provide opportunities for young people to explore their spirituality and their place in the world, and build positive relationships they can rely on.

We are now half way through our 2015-18 strategic plan, which set out three key objectives: to continue to increase the quality of our work; to strengthen our organisation; and to secure the long-term future of the work of Club. We have made solid progress on all three fronts, as you will see from this report.

The entire team has worked extremely hard over the year and we have seen the fruits of this. More children and young people are attending club; and the activities they attend are of higher quality. We are attracting new funding in an extremely difficult environment, and have made a small surplus on the year. To strengthen our strategic and operational capacity we have agreed to join the Worth Unlimited network.

The work of Club would not be possible without our volunteers, staff, supporters and funders, to whom we are incredibly grateful. We are very privileged to be able to work with the children, young people and families of South Kilburn, to be a part of the growth and change we see, and to be changed ourselves.

Matt Parker, Chair.

Quality Youth Work

Our first strategic objective is to continue to invest in the quality of our work. We have sought to embed good practices in our work, and to develop ways to understand and reflect on the impact we have.

A Story ~ Part 1 ~ Introducing Princess

Princess (name changed) is 9 years old and comes from an East African background. She attends a nearby mainstream primary school along with her brother. Princess's early interactions with us came as a result of her younger brother's regular attendance at our Junior after-school sessions.

Initially, although interested in coming to see what her brother does, she was shy and did not interact with the leaders or children. Often she would disappear into another room and sometimes eat other children's snacks without permission (much to the annoyance of the owner of the snacks!), or make a mess of other children's art works. She went through a phase of spitting and hitting out at children who she didn't understand when challenged or played with.

~ ~ ~

This has been reflected in on-going growth in the numbers and attendance rates of the children and young people. During the year we worked with 285 different children and young people. We ran 307 sessions which lasted for a total of 639 hours. We had 3,580 ticks on the register during that time. Just over half of these attendances were at our children's sessions. This is a 40% increase in attendance levels over the previous year.

We have continued to run the evening youth sessions, on Tuesday, Wednesday and Thursday evenings. We have experimented during the year with different structures. There is no longer a girls session, but we offer a more focussed activity session on Wednesdays, where there is a craft, or cooking, or some other project that is the main focus of the session.

To enable all of this to happen, there were approximately 2000 hours of face-to-face volunteering youth and children's work, by 18 different volunteers. This doesn't include all the planning and preparation time they put in, nor time spent by Trustees.

London Federation Quality Mark

We have continued to work towards achieving the bronze Quality Mark award. This has been led by Matt Perry, our Operations Manager. We are continuing to gather the evidence for the accreditation, which we now hope to achieve by the summer 2017, and also to build in processes to ensure the improvements we have seen are long-lasting.

Equipping the Team

As part of our ongoing commitment to staff development and training we have continued to train and support our staff and volunteers to help them improve their youth and children's work practice. Frontier Youth Trust provide regular training sessions, and volunteers receive support from the external placement partners. We have also offered work-based support to our full-time staff.

Volunteer Partnerships

This year we welcomed a new group of full- and part-time volunteers to the team. Stephania joined us from Colombia via Time For God. Nelson also comes from Colombia, via a new partnership with ICYE (Inter-Cultural Youth Exchange). Lea arrived from Berlin on the long-standing scheme with St Luke's and the Diocese of Berlin.

A Story ~ Part 2 ~ Joining In

To help bridge these common misunderstandings we wanted to encourage the children to overcome their reluctance to play with Princess. Our efforts to get her involved in the main games we played in the sports hall didn't quite work, and so we adopted a new approach. A member of our Junior team played with Princess at the side of the sports hall as the main games were going on, initiating a throwing game that she wanted to play with a soft ball. Over the months this allowed Princess to decide what she wanted to do, but also gently encouraged her to play with other children. We had a few other less active and shyer members of our Junior sessions, and so we gradually incorporated them into her self-initiated basketball type game. The children have come to understand her more and often play with her and involve her in what they do.

~ ~ ~

Last year we initiated a Parish Interns project with the Diocese of London. This provides young adults considering ordination with an opportunity to work in a parish in London. Interns join the community at Christian Holt House, and part of their placement

includes helping at two sessions/week at Club. As well as training provided by Club, volunteers receive support from the Diocese during the year.

Theory of Change and Impact

This year we have introduced a new way of understanding our work and its impact. At our annual planning weekend, Trustees, staff and volunteers worked together to think through what we do, and the difference it makes. Facilitated by Debbie Garden, from Frontier Youth Trust, we looked at the Huskins model of Youth Achievement.

We have adapted this slightly to our own circumstances, and after every session the team identify the step, and any evidence, that each young person is on. This then feeds into our reflection and planning processes.

A Story ~ Part 3 ~ Belonging

As the main games went on in the hall, each week the group went to do a small group game or a craft activity together. Princess regularly got involved, and started to lead on a few games. Over the course of the next few months she built some strong friendships during the games and activities. As her confidence grew, she started to join in the computer games without any encouragement from us. She was sitting down attentively taking tuition on the Xbox control from an older member of our Juniors, who patiently showed her how to play a co-operative fantasy game called Skylanders.

Princess still has her moments of not listening and behaving poorly to others, but now, she does say sorry and even gives hugs to the child she has accidentally upset.

Over the course of the year that we've known her, Princess has settled in really well and we've seen real change in her self-confidence and ability to relate positively to the other children and leaders. On the days we don't have Junior Club, Princess regularly comes past our front door on her scooter to say hello to us and see if her friends are in.

~ ~ ~

Brent funding – Sports & Health project

Our application to the Brent Council VSIF (Voluntary Sector Initiatives Fund) was successful (only 1 of 11 to be funded in the Borough – an indication of the current  funding situation). We will receive £45,000 over 2 years to run a Health and Sports project. This funding has allowed us to recruit a new full-time youth worker, and Lowell Weir will be joining the team in April 2017. The project aims to improve the health and well-being of the children and young people we work with, using both traditional team sports but also through non-competitive physical activities. It will also enable us to work with Disability Sports, a charity that provides sports training for children and young people with disabilities.

As the only full-time qualified member of staff, Stuart has done amazing work, but has been spread thin. Securing this funding will allow us to put more resources into our youth work in order to increase the quantity and range of youth work that we do.

A Story ~ Part 4 ~ What can we learn?

Princess' story highlights some key points about the OK Club

≈   We see real change in the lives of the children and young people. Over the course of the year Princess and the other children have been helped to understand each other.
≈   Change takes time, consistency and patience. And people – we rely on volunteers so that we have enough people that we can take time with a particular child to respond to their situation. And they need the support of skilled staff.
≈   Change is often planned and deliberate. The team take time outside of the main sessions to reflect on the individual children and young people and our work with them.
≈   There is always more to the games and activities than meets the eye. A visitor might come to club and see a ball game and think nothing more of it. But the ball game was a vital first step for Princess and the other children.

~ ~ ~

Building our capacity

Our second objective has been to build our organisational capacity in various ways.

Strategic Partnership to strengthen the organisation

Over the last couple of years we have approached a number of organisations to explore closer partnership working, in order to increase our organisational capacity and resilience. We sought larger youth organisations with compatible values, in order to look at different partnership models, up to and including mergers.

After a deliberately slow and considered process, we have now decided to join the Worth Unlimited network of organisations. This will enable us to retain our identity, independence and rootedness, while benefitting from the strategic and youth work support they can offer.

Financial Position

We are very pleased that we have been able to show a small surplus on the accounts in the 2016-17 financial year, for the first time for a few years. Summary accounts are below at page 13, and full accounts on our website.

The Trustees conducted a funding review of the organisation during the year. We have successfully increased our income from renting parts of our premises over the last year, to other community organisations with compatible aims and services.

Despite securing the funding from Brent Council, continued and deepening austerity policies across the public sector means we do not feel it likely that public funding for youth work will be available. We also recognise that we have limited resources to devote to fundraising. The priorities for the coming year are:

- Further increase income from premises hire
- Strengthen relationships with existing funders
- Improve our communications with, and growth of our individual supporter base

Long term sustainability

The existing fabric of the buildings that Club operates in (both the Club building/hall and the volunteer accommodation block) is tired and towards the end of its economic life. The Trustees remain of the view that developing our site will be the best use of our assets to secure the work of Club in the long term. To this end we have been in discussion with various partners to take this forward.

Our objectives in redeveloping the site are:

1. Provide high quality youth and children's work space (around 310 sq m)
2. Provide volunteer accommodation (for 12 people)
3. Provide a long-term, secure income stream sufficient to support the core activities of Club.

During the year we worked with Dolphin Living, who carried out a feasibility study of the site. This confirmed that our objectives are ambitious but achievable.

Any scheme will need the close co-operation of Brent Council; while we own the freehold to the main Club buildings, the other two-thirds of the site are on a leasehold, with Brent as the freeholder. We are in discussions with Brent Council now to explore how we might take this forward with them.

As this opportunity unfolds, we are also contacting other youth organisations to see if we can provide space for them alongside our own in any new scheme.

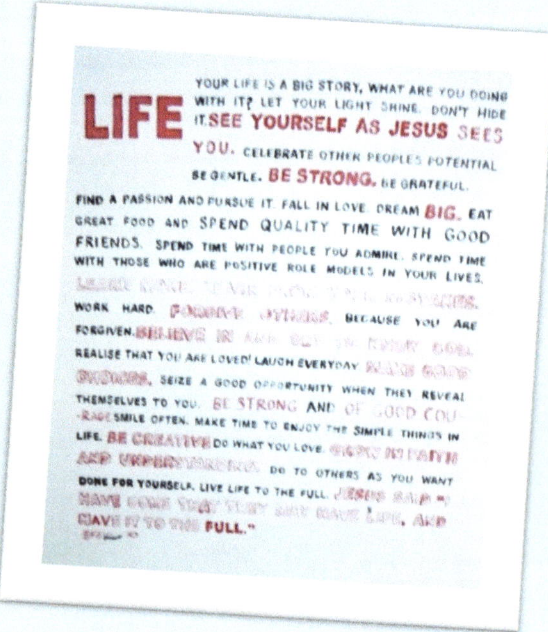

Summary Accounts

In the year to 31st March 2017 our total income was £96,021, and expenditure £94,296. This is a much improved position from previous years. We have managed to spend a little less, and raise more. Income from grants and donations is higher, as is that from renting out parts of the building to other community groups.

Full accounts are available from our website and the Charity Commission.

Statement of Financial Activities for the year to 31ˢᵗ March 2017

	Unrestricted funds	Restricted funds	2017 Total funds	2016 Total funds
	£	£	£	£
Income & Endowments from				
Donations and legacies	3,830	-	3,380	23,449
Charitable activities - operation of Club	58,790	33,350	92,140	48,868
Investment income	51	-	51	102
Total	**62,671**	**33,350**	**96,021**	**72,419**
Expenditure on				
Raising funds	544	-	544	516
Charitable activities - operation of Club	42,857	50,895	93,752	99,675
Total	**43,401**	**50,895**	**94,296**	**100,191**
Net Income / (Expenditure)	19,270	(17,545)	1,725	(27,772)

Balance Sheet as at 31st March 2017

	Unrestricted funds £	Restricted funds £	2017 Total funds £	2016 Total funds £
Fixed Assets				
Tangible assets	-	691,164	691,164	708,709
Current Assets				
Cash at bank	53,001	3,438	56,439	37,858
Creditors				
Amounts falling due within 1 year	(9,241)	(1)	(9,242)	(9,931)
Net Current Assets	**43,760**	**3,437**	**47,197**	**27,927**
Total Assets less Current Liabilities	43,760	694,601	738,361	736,636
Net Assets	**43,760**	**694,601**	**738,361**	**736,636**
Funds				
Unrestricted funds			43,760	24,490
Restricted funds			694,601	712,146
Total Funds			**738,361**	**736,636**

We would like to thank all those that support the work of the OK Club: our volunteers and parents; the individuals and churches that regularly support our work financially; and our current larger funders - John Lyon's Charity, the Girdler's Company, and Brent Council.